A Special Day

Sally Odgers

Illustrated by Gaston Vanzet

Today is a special day!
Today is festival day.

"It's time to get up," says Mom.

I put on my special clothes.

"It's time to go to town," says Dad.
I pick up my trumpet.

"It's time to start!" says Mr. Cruz.

I play my trumpet.

"It's time to stop," says Mr. Cruz.
I hear the people clap!

"It's time to go home," says Dad.
I say goodbye to Mr. Cruz.

13

"It's time to go to bed," Mom says.
I say, "Good night."

MAR
FEST
Town
Saturday

Today was a special day.
Today was festival day.